GUNTER'S GLORIOUS
PRANK
JOURNAL

by Kirsten Mayer
illustrated by Zachary Sterling

CARTOON
NETWORK™
B O O K S

An Imprint of Penguin Random House

CARTOON NETWORK BOOKS
Penguin Young Readers Group
An Imprint of Penguin Random House LLC

Penguin supports copyright. Copyright fuels creativity, encourages diverse
voices, promotes free speech, and creates a vibrant culture. Thank you for
buying an authorized edition of this book and for complying with copyright
laws by not reproducing, scanning, or distributing any part of it in any form
without permission. You are supporting writers and allowing Penguin to
continue to publish books for every reader.

ADVENTURE TIME, CARTOON NETWORK, the logos and all related
characters and elements are trademarks of and © Cartoon Network. (s16).

Published in 2016 by Cartoon Network Books, an imprint of Penguin Random
House LLC, 345 Hudson Street, New York, New York 10014.
Printed in the USA.

ISBN 978-0-8431-8344-3   10 9 8 7 6 5 4 3 2 1

This pranktastic journal belongs to:

~~GUNTER~~

Just kidding! It really belongs to:

Miguel B

Gunter is making some kind of top secret potion! Fill in the rest of his recipe:

1 whole _____
10 chopped _____
2 cups of _____
1 dozen _____
1/4 cup _____
3 teaspoons _____
Dash of freshly ground _____
Generous pinch of _____

WENK!
WENK!

1. Mix together the _____,
_____, and
_____ in a large pot.
Heat the mixture until it turns a bright
_____ color and smells like
_____.
2. Add the _____ and
_____, then set aside to
cool for _____ minutes.
3. In a separate dish, mash the
_____ and
_____ into a thick paste,
then sprinkle _____ all
over the top.
4. Combine in a blender until it turns into a
fizzy liquid.
5. Serve!

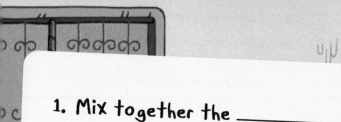

That Gunter better not be out much longer!

Peppermint Butler comes along and takes a sip.

Excuse me! Science, you lab rat, you played a prank on me!

Squeak! Squeak!

PRANK ALERT!

Spoil someone's morning juice with a cheesy surprise! Orange cheese powder from a mac-and-cheese packet will color water to look like OJ!

PRANK ALERT!

You can play this same prank by gluing some coins to the sidewalk, especially quarters! Watch people try to pick them up! Note: Do this outside, not in your house. Gluing stuff to your own floor is dumb.

PRANK ALERT!

Disorient your BFF by setting his or her alarm to go off thirty minutes earlier.
It will make their whole day feel off!

The Gunters communicate in their own wenky language. Write out a translation of their phone conversation!

Gunter #1:
_____

Gunter #2:
_____

Gunter #1:
_____

Gunter #2:
_____

Gunter #1:
_____

Gunter #2:
_____

Hey, who are you talking to? Get back here! I need you to curl my beard!

Rate these dishes:
1 for YUCK, 5 for EGGSTRAORDINARY, and
for WHAT THE EGG IS THAT?

Cheesy omelet	1	2	3	4	5
Meaty omelet	1	2	3	4	5
Fried eggs	1	2	3	4	5
Scrambled eggs	1	2	3	4	5
Egg-drop soup	1	2	3	4	5
Quiche	1	2	3	4	5
Deviled eggs	1	2	3	4	5
Matzah brei	1	2	3	4	5
Custard	1	2	3	4	5
Egg in a basket	1	2	3	4	5
Eggs Benedict	1	2	3	4	5
Huevos rancheros	1	2	3	4	5
Egg salad	1	2	3	4	5
Pickled eggs	1	2	3	4	5
Meringue	1	2	3	4	5
Tofu eggless eggs	1	2	3	4	5

The Jelly Bean People come in and get the eggs, carting them off to the Royal Tartorium.
The Jelly Bean People try to bake tarts in the Royal Tartorium, but all the eggs are hard-boiled! What an eggs-ellent prank!

PRANK ALERT!

Hard-boil all the eggs, place them back in the egg carton, and return them to the fridge. Everyone will get a big surprise the next time they try to bake or make some scrambled eggs!

Bean Boxing

Grab a friend and take turns drawing a straight line across or down between two Jelly Bean People. The goal is to complete a square. When you do, color in your box with one color. If you finish a box, you get to take another turn. Your friend should fill in his or her boxes with another color, or it will get super weird! When it's all colored in, count up your boxes. Whoever has the most is the winner!

The Jelly Bean People feel like pranking it forward. They can't bake tarts without eggs, so instead they cut sponges into tart shapes. Then they decorate the sponges to look like tarts!

PRANK ALERT!

Cut up a sponge and then frost it like a cake. Watch your friends try to cut into it!

Decorate these treats with some fun frosting designs!

PRANK ALERT!

It's easy to short-sheet a bed and make someone think their bed shrank! Pull back the covers and take the top flat sheet off the bed. Place the sheet over the head of the bed, where the pillows go, and tuck it in all around (like you normally would at the foot of the bed). Then fold the bottom half of the sheet back up toward the head, and leave it untucked. Pull the covers over it like normal. When someone gets into bed, they won't be able to fit, and will have to make their bed all over again!

IMPORTANT NEWS!

Folks will believe anything they read! Write a fake news story and add a picture of something totally unbelievable. Make sure to interview lots of fake "sources" for your article.

Turtle Princess also wants to prank it forward. She makes a special treat to give to Tree Trunks: a mayonnaise-filled doughnut! It looks just like a regular doughnut, but it sure doesn't taste like one!

Tree Trunks asks Turtle Princess to help her make some "treats" for her one true love, Mr. Pig. They get to work making toothpaste cookies and a basketful of caramel-covered onions!

PRANK ALERT!

Nothing startles someone like biting into something that tastes different from what he or she expected!

- Stick a lollipop stick into a peeled onion, and dip it into melted caramel. It will look just like a caramel apple.

- Take the crème filling out of some sandwich cookies, and replace it with a smear of toothpaste. Put the cookies back together and serve with milk!

- Get some filled doughnuts. Fill a pastry bag with mayonnaise. Carefully jab the tip into the doughnut and slowly squeeze mayonnaise into the pastry, as much as you can before it starts coming out of the doughnut!

Tree Trunks puts a bunch of caramel onions in a basket and delivers them to Mr. Pig.

A candy apple? For me? Why, thank you, my darling.

Why hello, Mr. Pig. I've brought you a nice and tasty treat.

Mr. Pig takes a big bite. "What?! I do believe that this apple has gone bad."
Tree Trunks laughs. "Haw-haw, I got you!"
Mr. Pig decides that a caramel-covered onion doesn't taste so bad after all, and he winds up eating the whole basket!

TIC-TAC-DOUGH

Challenge a friend to a game of Tic-Tac-Dough. One of you should be X and one of you should be O (like doughnuts). Take turns drawing an X or O in each space until one of you gets three across, down, or diagonally!

PRANK ALERT!

People just grab their bags and go, without checking everything inside. Put some rocks in a bag to make it strangely heavy. Throw a few plastic spiders in there for a random surprise later when they get pulled out. Or lock the zipper pulls! (Note: You better have the key handy in case they need to do some homework!)

JOKER'S WILD!

You can tell your friend a joke that takes a REALLY long time, and then annoy them with the punch line. First, pick a color. Then write out a story with that color, like this: Once upon a time, there was a pink person, who lived in a pink one-story house, with pink windows, pink shutters, and a pink door. Inside the house there was a pink table, a pink chair, a pink lamp, a pink refrigerator, and a pink sofa . . . You get the idea. Then always end the joke with "What color were the stairs?" The person will guess pink, and you can say, "There weren't any stairs. It's a one-story house!"

Pick a color and write out your joke here:
Once upon a time, there was a/an _____ person
who lived in a/an _____ one-story house . . .

_____

_____

_____

_____

_____

_____

_____

_____

_____

_____

_____

_____

_____

Wildberry Princess lifts the lid from the box . . . and screams.
"EEEEEEEEEEE! It's a finger! It's a finger! GROSS!"
Mr. Cupcake pulls out his hand and wriggles his fingers.
"Relax! I pranked ya!"

PRANK ALERT!

Fool your friends by wriggling your finger around inside a gift box! Simply cut a hole in the bottom of a box and grab some tissue paper. Stick your thumb or finger up into the box, and nestle it on the tissue paper. Add a bit of red nail polish, ketchup, or chalky powder for an extra-dead look. Don't forget to offer to hold the gift while they open it. Works best with a box that has a lid instead of something you have to wrap.

The princesses decide to prank their friends back by changing their voicemails. Record a message that sounds like you answered the phone to fake out your friends—or make it sound like they reached a wrong number!

PRANK ALERT!

Record yourself as if you were answering the phone and then having a conversation. Or record a wrong-number message in your best automaton voice.

Here are some examples of fake voicemails:

1. Hey, what's up? (pause.) Yeah. (pause) Uh-huh. (pause.) That sounds cool! (pause.) Hey, guess what? This is my voicemail, I'm not really here right now!
2. We're sorry. The number you have reached has been disconnected. Good-bye.

Write more ideas here for different fake voicemails!

_____

_____

_____

_____

_____

_____

_____

_____

_____

_____

_____

Meanwhile, back at the castle, Gunter watches all the pranks happening on the security cameras and loves it! He sends out all the other Gunters with more Prank Potion, to spread even more chaos.

GUNTERMANIA

Fill these pages with Gunters.

Finn, Jake, and BMO keep looking for Princess Bubblegum, but they can't find her anywhere. A laughing Banana Guard says she might be in the dungeon, so the heroes set off to look for her.

SECRET PASSAGE

Find the path through this maze to get to the dungeon!

PRANK ALERT!

Pretend you see some food on someone's face, or a bug on their shoulder. Keep pointing it out, and it will drive them crazy as they try to wipe it off!

Why are these eggs so sweet? And why are my waffles so salty?

PRANK ALERT!

A trick as old as time: Put sugar in the saltshaker, and salt in the sugar bowl.

EEK! Who did this to the sink? I'm gonna get all soggy!

PRANK ALERT!

Rig the kitchen sink with duct tape to give somebody a surprise shower! Carefully put some duct tape over the bottom of the kitchen faucet, sealing the back and sides, but leaving open the very front for water to shoot through. The next time someone turns on the faucet, they'll get sprayed in the face. Sit back and watch the waterworks!

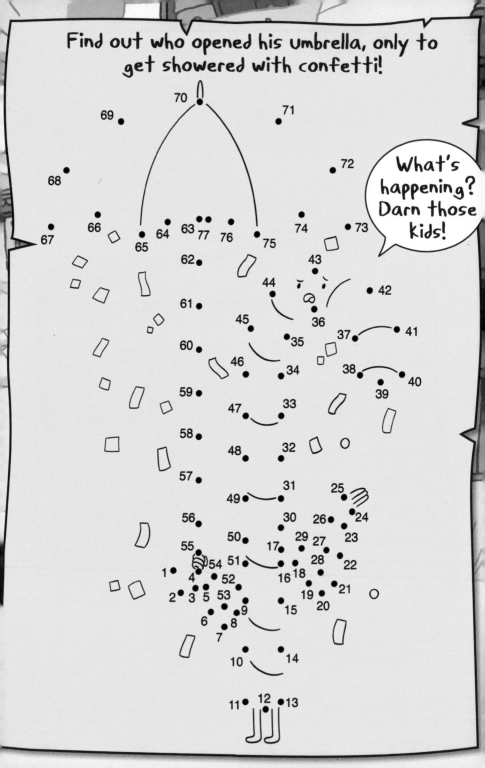

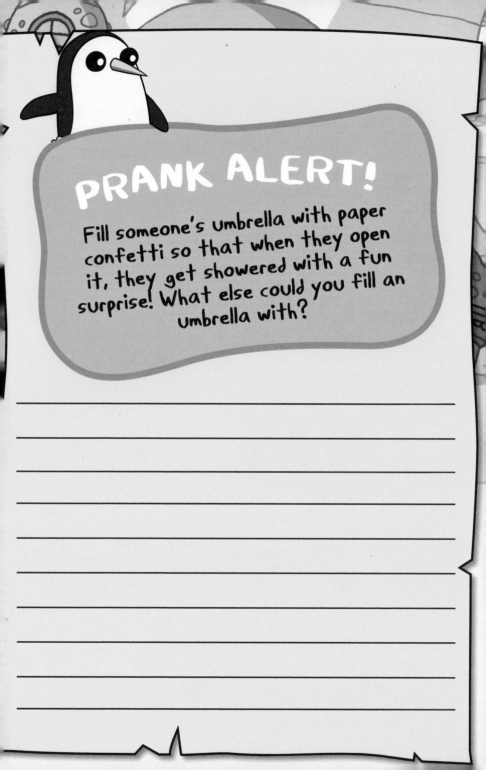

PRANK ALERT!

Fill someone's umbrella with paper confetti so that when they open it, they get showered with a fun surprise! What else could you fill an umbrella with?

_____

_____

_____

_____

_____

_____

_____

_____

_____

_____

PRANK ALERT!

If you stuff some cotton balls into your friends' shoes, they will think their shoes are suddenly too small!

Where in the Castle Is Princess Bubblegum?

Find all these words in the word-search box. Write down the remaining letters from left to right in the spaces below. It will spell out where she is!

Amber Prison

Bedroom

Grand Hall

Closet

Dungeon

Science Lab

Secret Room

Nursery

Tea Room

Bathroom

Hallway

The Tree

Royal Tartortium

Kitchen

_____ _____

__ _____ ____ ___ ____

_____, _____ _____. ____

___ _____ _____ __

___ _____ ___ ___ _____

___ _____ ___ ___ ____

_____ _____.

P R I N C E S B S B U B B L E G
N U M I S R E E L A X I N G W I
U G R A N D H A L L T H H E R B
R E S T R H A L L W A Y F R I E
S N D O L A D Y R A I N I C D O
E R O Y A L T A R T O R T I U M
R M R N T H E Y A R E S S B N U
Y N N I T E S O L C N C G A G T
H M O O R A E T E M S I E T E L
V M O O R T E R C E S E E H O E
K I T C H E N S O N T N H R N E
E R O O F O F T H E C C A O N R
A M B E R P R I S O N E D O Y T
C A S T L E A N D D R L I M N E
K I N G H O T T E A F A R O M H
C A N D I E D T E A C B U P S T

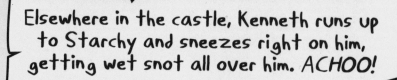

Elsewhere in the castle, Kenneth runs up to Starchy and sneezes right on him, getting wet snot all over him. *ACHOO!*

Oh noooo! Now I'm gonna get the zombie sickness again!

PRANK ALERT!

Use a juice box to pretend to sneeze all over someone. Point the juice box's straw at your victim. Then, fake-sneeze very dramatically, squeezing the juice box at the same time. They'll think you sneezed all over them! Gross!

Starchy runs to see Nurse Pound Cake, and after she gives him a clean bill of health, he slides a whoopee cushion into her chair. When the nurse sits down...

BLFFFFFT!

Starchy's feeling healthy again! And a bit too pranky, if you ask me.

PRANK ALERT!

Whoopee cushions make loud noises when you sit on them. It's best to slip them under a cushion or blanket so they aren't spotted.

Slammin' Storytime

Write a story about a prank. Think up some of the story details first.

_____ plays a prank on _____,
who is his/her_____.
The prank is_____.
The prankee reacts by_____ and
saying "_____."
Okay, now write out the story! Write a beginning, a middle, and an end! Don't forget the HA-HA-HAs!

_____

_____

_____

_____

_____

_____

_____

_____

_____

_____

_____

The End!

Princess Bubblegum takes the gang to the lab to work on an antidote, but one ingredient is still missing. Just then, Peppermint Butler brings them a snack!
This milk has chunks in it! That ain't cool, man.
PRANK ALERT!
Put a bunch of mini marshmallows into a glass of milk, and serve. The drinker will think it went bad and has chunks in it!

Wait, that's it! My prank antidote needs marshmallows as its final ingredient.

List the rest of the ingredients in Princess Bubblegum's Prankidote!

_____

_____

_____

_____

_____

_____

The Gumball Guardians travel around the Candy Kingdom, spraying the antidote over all its citizens. The reign of random pranking is over!

Mathematical! How many Gunters did Finn and Jake round up in the Candy Castle? Count them.

Lemongrab finds a diary in the woods. Inside, it says that the owner has hidden her most precious possession somewhere out there. There's a map to follow where X marks the spot.
What's this rigamarole? I must find out.
Lemongrab searches day and night, digging holes all over the forest, until he finally digs up a box that looks like a treasure chest. He holds his breath and opens it to find . . . a note that reads:

Think up some more pranktastic pranks to play. Write them down here!

_____

_____

_____

_____

_____

_____

_____

_____

_____

_____

_____

_____

_____

_____

Dear _____,

I'd like to apologize for the recent prank I played on you— a little something I like to call _____. It was all meant in good fun. Please feel free to play a prank on me in the future as fair retribution. Below is a list of suggestions, to make your life easier.

Pranks you might play on me:

1. _____
2. _____
3. _____

Sincerely,
Prankmaster

_____